HISTORY'S MYSTERIES!
DINOSAURS
Activity Book

GEORGE TOUFEXIS

DOVER PUBLICATIONS
Garden City, New York

Bibliographical Note

History's Mysteries! Dinosaurs Activity Book is a new work,
first published by Dover Publications in 2012.

International Standard Book Number

ISBN-13: 978-0-486-48698-7
ISBN-10: 0-486-48698-2

Printed in the United States of America
48698207
www.doverpublications.com

INTRODUCTION

Probably the greatest of History's Mysteries is the lost world of the dinosaurs. What were these creatures really like? Since they no longer exist, we can only guess—but with the evidence available to us, we can make some pretty good guesses! In this book you'll find many amazing facts about the dinosaurs.

  Explore some of the biggest mysteries: Did they really disappear or do they still exist in some forgotten jungle—or deep in the ocean? Scientists are still hard at work digging up and studying fossils. In fact, some of the mysteries and questions in this book may be answered before you finish reading!

THE WORLD OF THE DINOSAURS

During the time of the dinosaurs, our world was very different. Here are two maps: one of our present world, and one believed by scientists to be what the Earth looked like in prehistoric times. How the land changed shape can give us clues as to what finally happened to the dinosaurs.

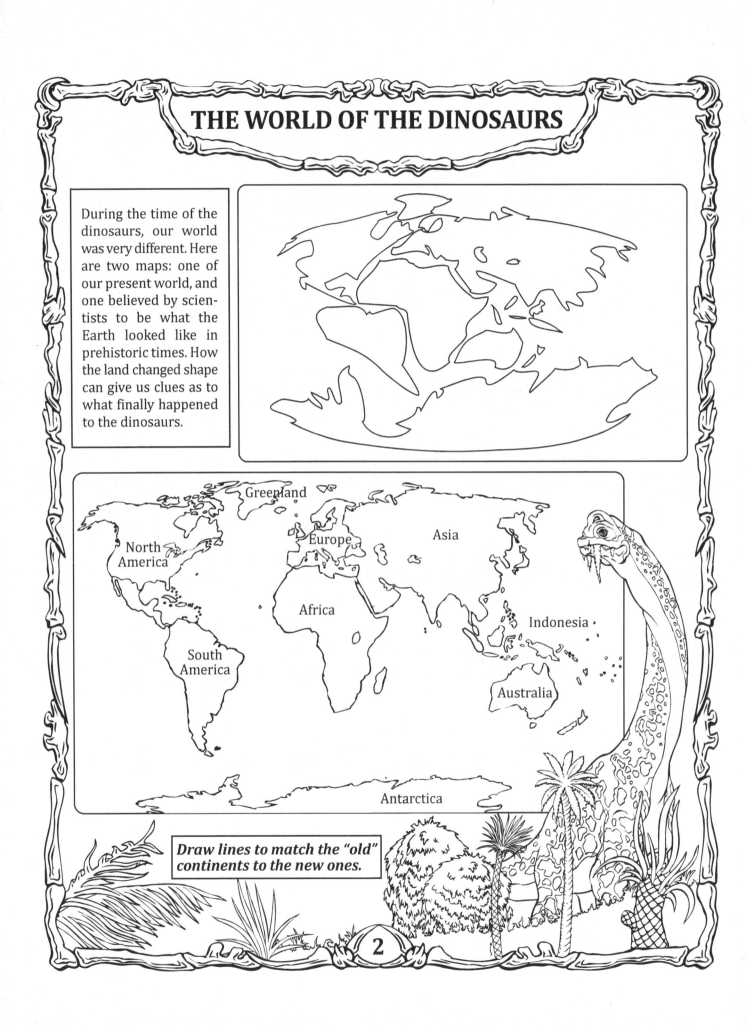

Greenland

North America

Europe

Asia

Africa

South America

Indonesia

Australia

Antarctica

Draw lines to match the "old" continents to the new ones.

CREATE YOUR OWN DINOSAUR!

How do we know what dinosaurs looked like? Scientists uncover fossils of dinosaur bones all over the world, but they have to imagine what the "outside" of a dinosaur looked like. Using fossils and information about modern animals (birds, amphibians, mammals, and reptiles), they put these amazing creatures together.

Can you draw what this predator may have looked like over the skeleton below?

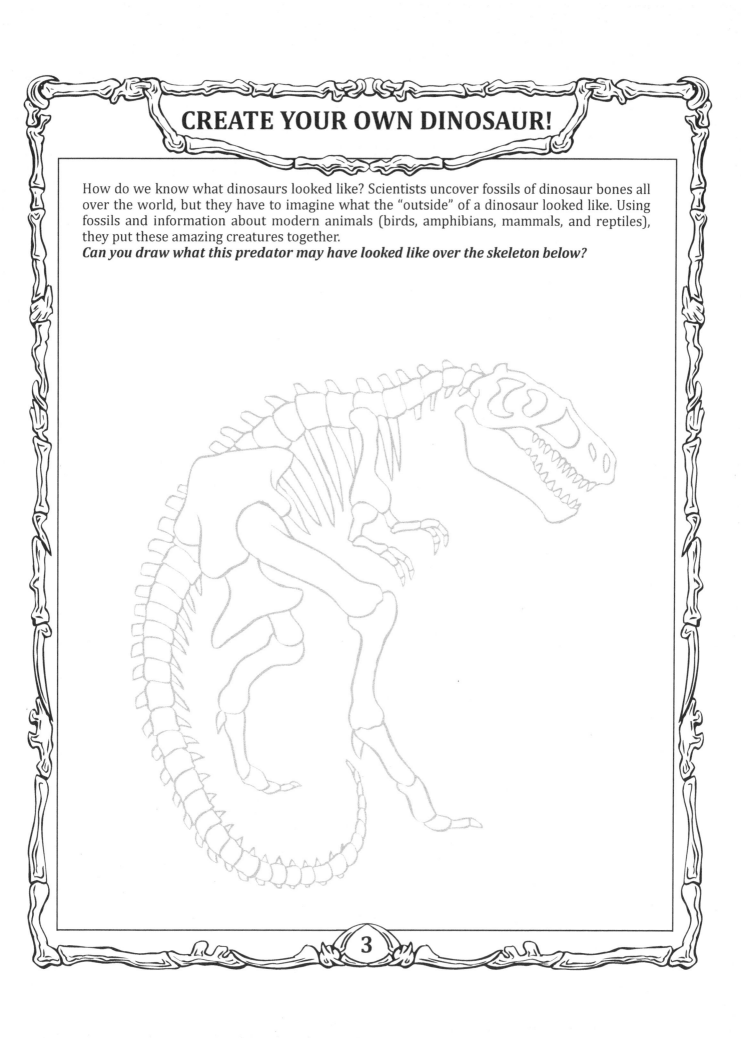

DINOSAUR FEATHERS?

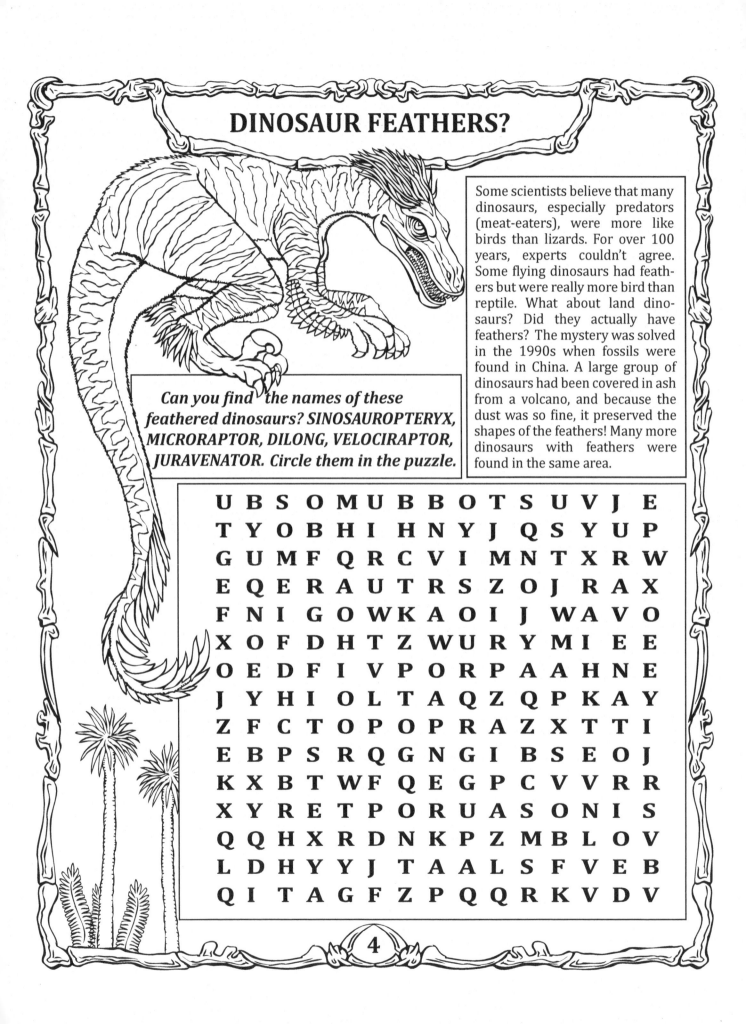

Some scientists believe that many dinosaurs, especially predators (meat-eaters), were more like birds than lizards. For over 100 years, experts couldn't agree. Some flying dinosaurs had feathers but were really more bird than reptile. What about land dinosaurs? Did they actually have feathers? The mystery was solved in the 1990s when fossils were found in China. A large group of dinosaurs had been covered in ash from a volcano, and because the dust was so fine, it preserved the shapes of the feathers! Many more dinosaurs with feathers were found in the same area.

Can you find the names of these feathered dinosaurs? SINOSAUROPTERYX, MICRORAPTOR, DILONG, VELOCIRAPTOR, JURAVENATOR. Circle them in the puzzle.

U B S O M U B B B O T S U V J E
T Y O B H I H N Y J Q S Y U P
G U M F Q R C V I M N T X R W
E Q E R A U T R S Z O J R A X
F N I G O W K A O I J W A V O
X O F D H T Z W U R Y M I E E
O E D F I V P O R P A A H N E
J Y H I O L T A Q Z Q P K A Y
Z F C T O P O P R A Z X T T I
E B P S R Q G N G I B S E O J
K X B T W F Q E G P C V V R R
X Y R E T P O R U A S O N I S
Q Q H X R D N K P Z M B L O V
L D H Y Y J T A A L S F V E B
Q I T A G F Z P Q Q R K V D V

WHAT COLOR WERE DINOSAURS?

One of the biggest mysteries about dinosaurs: What color were they?

Scientists guessed that dinosaurs were the same color as modern lizards and reptiles—until they did some testing of a fossil of Sinosauropteryx. They found that this creature was bright red and orange!

Keep those colors in mind as you color this scene.

HOW DID ~~~~ SO BIG?

One of the most puzzling dinosaur mysteries is their size. How did they get so big? It's a tough question, but some scientists have suggested these ideas about size:

IDEA 1: Dinosaurs got big because of food.

Temperatures were much warmer in prehistoric times. The Earth was covered with all kinds of plants. The largest dinosaurs were plant eaters and may have become huge over time because there was so much food. This would also explain why most meat eaters got so big: you'd have to be big to take down a 50-ton plant eater!

IDEA 2: The largest dinosaurs survived because of their size.

Some scientists think that over a long time, the larger dinosaurs, that were not hunted by predators as much, just kept getting bigger—That is, until the predators got bigger!

IDEA 3: Dinosaurs were able to get big because of their body temperature.

Some scientists believe that if the dinosaurs were cold-blooded (their body temperature was affected by the weather), a very large dinosaur could warm up in the sun during the day and cool down at night very slowly, giving it an even body temperature all the time. That way, the larger ones would survive the temperature changes better than the smaller ones.

6

HOW DID THEY GET SO BIG?

On the left are the names of some of the biggest dinosaurs. Unscramble the names on the right and match them.

ARGENTINOSAURUS   RHOUATTARP

SAUROPOSEIDON   ONESPRODIOSUA

SPINOSAURUS   ITOEUARURNGSSAN

QUETZALCOATLUS   OUANUSSSPIR

LIOPLEURODON   OSQLTAUULCETAZ

SHANTUNGOSAURUS   IOOONLLDUERP

UTAHRAPTOR   UASNTHOAGNSUSUR

SHONISAURUS   RSSNAOUUISH

Human, 6 feet tall

DINOSAUR SKIN

What was dinosaur skin like? Many years ago, experts thought it was made up of scales, like fish or snakes. Then, scientists found a nearly complete skeleton of a Carnotaurus (meaning "meat-bull" because of its two thick horns above the eyes that made it look somewhat like a bull). They were able to see a pattern of skin along one side, so we have a much better idea of what dinosaur skin looked like.

```
E L M S U R U A S A C U A P
W M D C R A J A S A U R U S
M A J U N G A S A U R U S L
T G X C O X N N M I E Z T B
B S Q T P T R U U N A X L W
S S U R U A S I L E B A C A
E E J K I P P A C I X V J R
E K M J I S M F Z B X R A A
W P D E U N Z T W G W I L N
L A M E T A S A U R U S F G
B A Q D Z I E W Y P Q X W D
C A R N O T A U R U S G G J
```

The CARNOTAURUS has some close relatives:
AUCASAURUS, MAJUNGASAURUS, ABELISAURUS,
RAJASAURUS, LAMETASAURUS
Can you find and circle their names?

LARGEST DINOSAUR EVER?

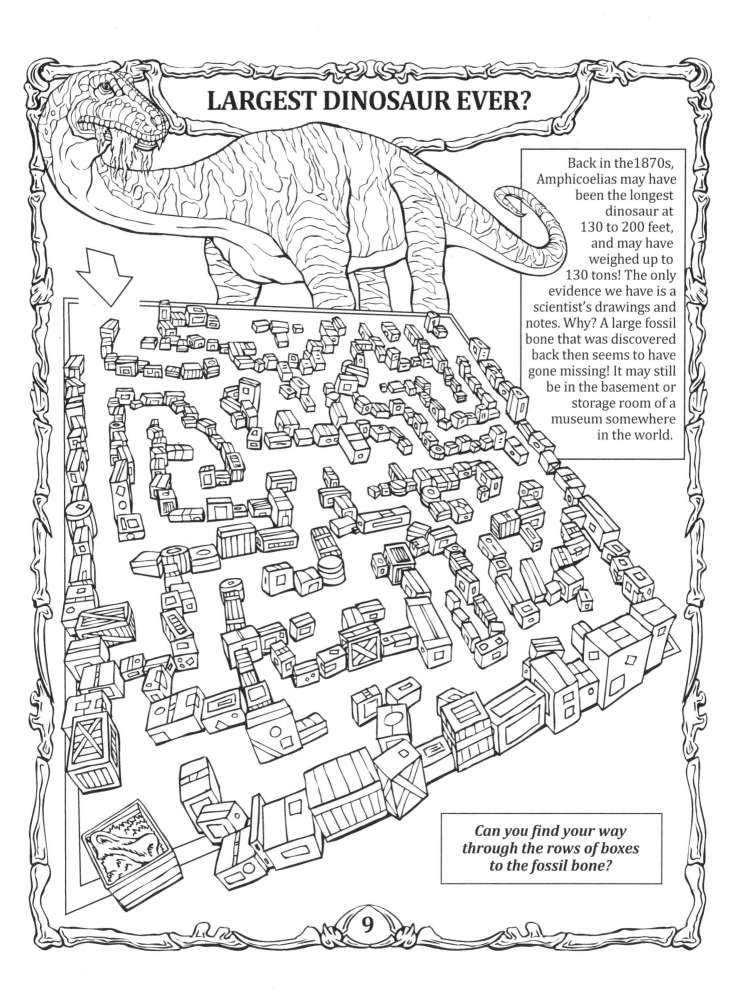

Back in the1870s, Amphicoelias may have been the longest dinosaur at 130 to 200 feet, and may have weighed up to 130 tons! The only evidence we have is a scientist's drawings and notes. Why? A large fossil bone that was discovered back then seems to have gone missing! It may still be in the basement or storage room of a museum somewhere in the world.

Can you find your way through the rows of boxes to the fossil bone?

DINOSAUR NAMES

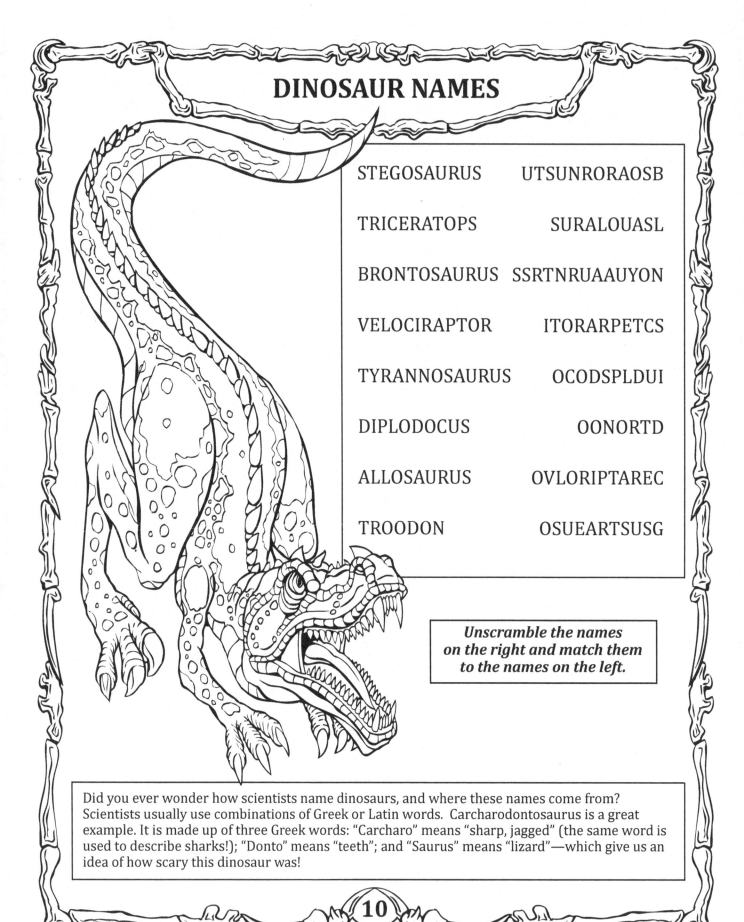

STEGOSAURUS	UTSUNROROAOSB
TRICERATOPS	SURALOUASL
BRONTOSAURUS	SSRTNRUAAUYON
VELOCIRAPTOR	ITORARPETCS
TYRANNOSAURUS	OCODSPLDUI
DIPLODOCUS	OONORTD
ALLOSAURUS	OVLORIPTAREC
TROODON	OSUEARTSUSG

Unscramble the names on the right and match them to the names on the left.

Did you ever wonder how scientists name dinosaurs, and where these names come from? Scientists usually use combinations of Greek or Latin words. Carcharodontosaurus is a great example. It is made up of three Greek words: "Carcharo" means "sharp, jagged" (the same word is used to describe sharks!); "Donto" means "teeth"; and "Saurus" means "lizard"—which give us an idea of how scary this dinosaur was!

THE BIGGEST PREDATOR OF THEM ALL?

It was thought that the Tyranno-saurus Rex was the biggest meat eater among the dinosaurs, until researchers found fossils of this beast! The Spinosaurus grew to almost 60 feet and weighed over 20 tons—plus it had an awe-some "sail" on its back.

ARE DINOSAURS STILL WITH US?

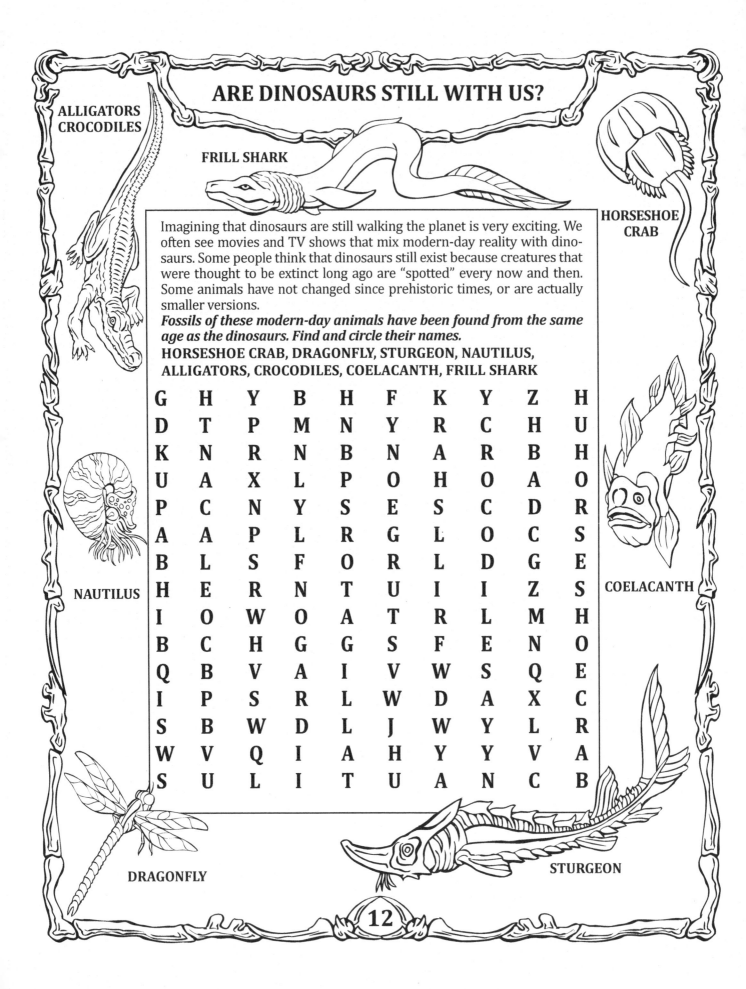

ALLIGATORS CROCODILES

FRILL SHARK

HORSESHOE CRAB

Imagining that dinosaurs are still walking the planet is very exciting. We often see movies and TV shows that mix modern-day reality with dinosaurs. Some people think that dinosaurs still exist because creatures that were thought to be extinct long ago are "spotted" every now and then. Some animals have not changed since prehistoric times, or are actually smaller versions.

Fossils of these modern-day animals have been found from the same age as the dinosaurs. Find and circle their names.

HORSESHOE CRAB, DRAGONFLY, STURGEON, NAUTILUS, ALLIGATORS, CROCODILES, COELACANTH, FRILL SHARK

G	H	Y	B	H	F	K	Y	Z	H
D	T	P	M	N	Y	R	C	H	U
K	N	R	N	B	N	A	R	B	H
U	A	X	L	P	O	H	O	A	O
P	C	N	Y	S	E	S	C	D	R
A	A	P	L	R	G	L	O	C	S
B	L	S	F	O	R	L	D	G	E
H	E	R	N	T	U	I	I	Z	S
I	O	W	O	A	T	R	L	M	H
B	C	H	G	G	S	F	E	N	O
Q	B	V	A	I	V	W	S	Q	E
I	P	S	R	L	W	D	A	X	C
S	B	W	D	L	J	W	Y	L	R
W	V	Q	I	A	H	Y	Y	V	A
S	U	L	I	T	U	A	N	C	B

NAUTILUS

COELACANTH

DRAGONFLY

STURGEON

SCARY SIGHTINGS!

Every now and then there are sightings of a giant creature that the observers believe to be a dinosaur. Here are a few examples, starting with Southeast Asia. Since the 1990s, a large creature has been sighted on islands above Papua New Guinea. The creature had a long tail and neck and was over 30 feet in length. It walked slowly on two legs and had smooth, shiny brown skin. The local people who saw it were shown a book of dinosaurs—and they pointed to a picture of a Therizinosaurus!

Here are 2 Therizinosaurus that seem to be identical.
Can you find and circle 11 differences?

13

MOKELE-MBEMBE

Mokele-Mbembe is the name of a large water creature, or spirit, in popular legends of the Congo River in Africa. Many expeditions went through uncharted Africa to find this mysterious creature. Some sightings report a dinosaur-like creature. Legends describe it as having an elephant-like body with a long neck and tail and a small head. Does it look familiar?

14

LOCH NESS MONSTER!

Many claim that the Loch Ness Monster, or "Nessie" is actually a big prehistoric sea creature. People have tried to find it, but without luck.

Here are six actual dinosaurs that lived in water and match the descriptions of "Nessie." One of them could still be doing the backstroke in the chilly waters of Scotland!
Find and circle these names in the puzzle:
ASKEPTOSAURUS, CRYPTOCLIDUS, GEOSAURUS, HOVASAURUS, PLESIOSAURUS, THILILUA

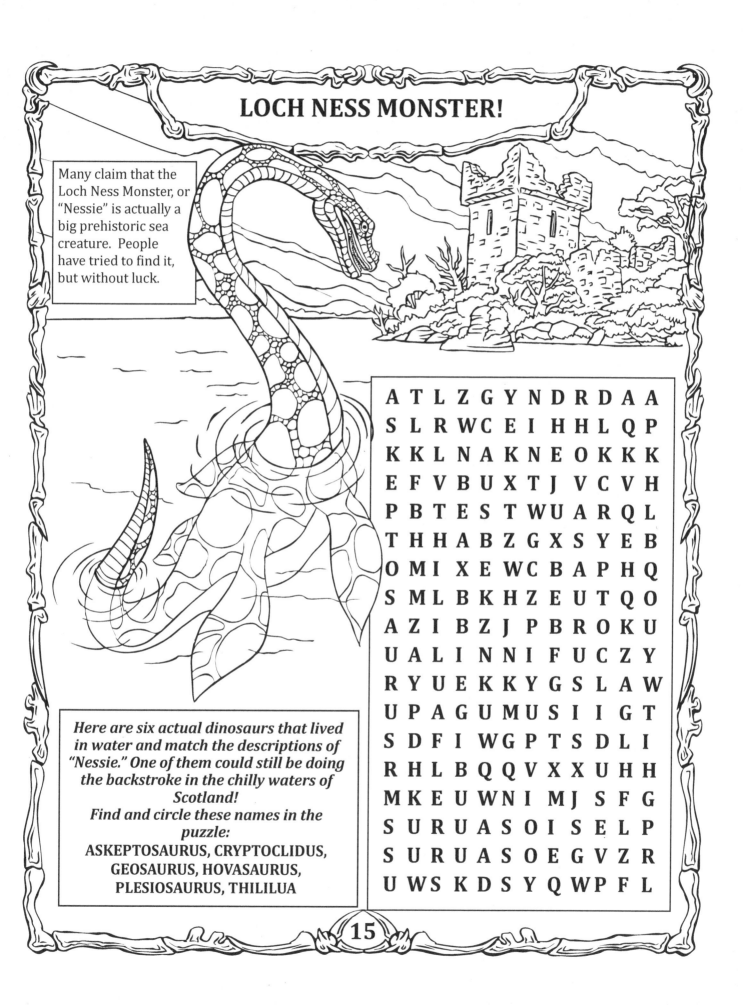

```
A T L Z G Y N D R D A A
S L R W C E I H H L Q P
K K L N A K N E O K K K
E F V B U X T J V C V H
P B T E S T W U A R Q L
T H H A B Z G X S Y E B
O M I X E W C B A P H Q
S M L B K H Z E U T Q O
A Z I B Z J P B R O K U
U A L I N N I F U C Z Y
R Y U E K K Y G S L A W
U P A G U M U S I I G T
S D F I W G P T S D L I
R H L B Q Q V X X U H H
M K E U W N I M J S F G
S U R U A S O I S E L P
S U R U A S O E G V Z R
U W S K D S Y Q W P F L
```

GIANT FLYERS

While exploring the Sonora Desert in Arizona in 1699, Conquistador Captain Juan Mateo Manje was told by the Pima Indians that a giant monster lived in a nearby cave. It was a menace to the Pima because it would fly around and catch as many people as it could eat! It's called Quetzalcoatlus by Mexicans and Thunderbird by Native Americans. Though thought to be a legend, there have been many recorded sightings of giant feathered birds and even skin-covered creatures.

Take a good look at this design. Now use your imagination and draw what you think they saw: a giant eagle? A pterodactyl?

DRAGONS

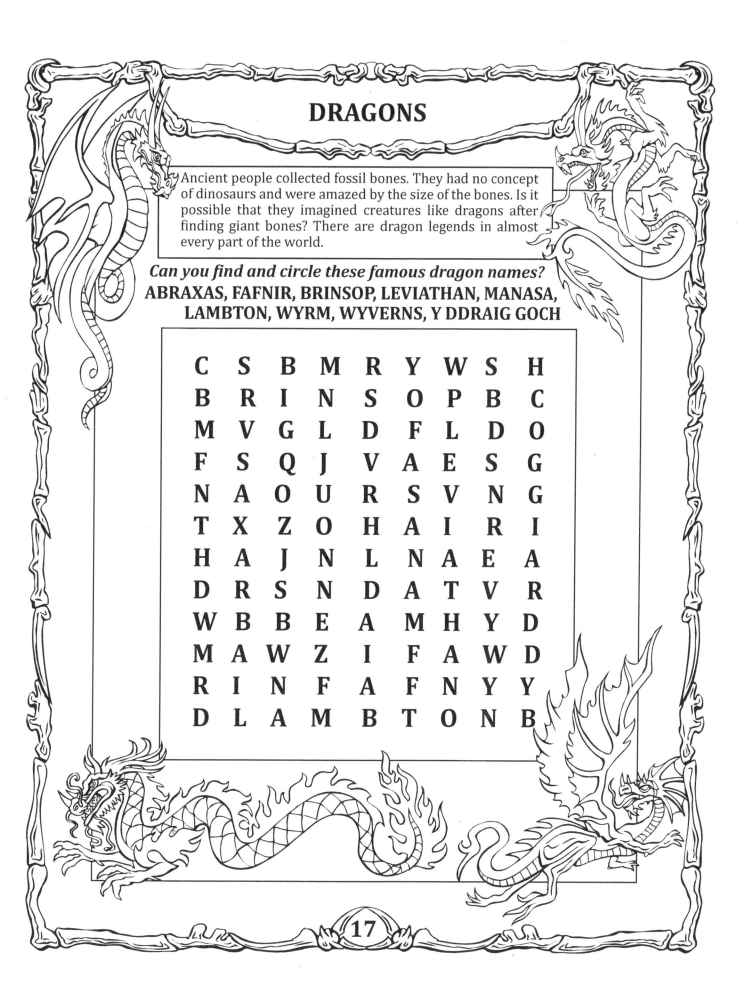

Ancient people collected fossil bones. They had no concept of dinosaurs and were amazed by the size of the bones. Is it possible that they imagined creatures like dragons after finding giant bones? There are dragon legends in almost every part of the world.

Can you find and circle these famous dragon names?
ABRAXAS, FAFNIR, BRINSOP, LEVIATHAN, MANASA, LAMBTON, WYRM, WYVERNS, Y DDRAIG GOCH

```
C S B M R Y W S H
B R I N S O P B C
M V G L D F L D O
F S Q J V A E S G
N A O U R S V N G
T X Z O H A I R I
H A J N L N A E A
D R S N D A T V R
W B B E A M H Y D
M A W Z I F A W D
R I N F A F N Y Y
D L A M B T O N B
```

SEA MONSTERS

Here's some names of sea monsters:
can you find and circle them?

CHARYBDIS, SEA MONK, TRUNKO, LUSCA, ZIPHIUS, KRAKEN, STEIPEREIDUR, SERPENT, KODIAK

```
S A V S B Z B V W S R Z
T F C P W T U T U E P S
W H Y S H L P E Z A T Q
I J I F U R E N B E C A
M E O Z A L E N I H D U
D X Q G I K I P A V T R
F X B U A C E R Z T F I
P Y T R X R Y H N C B H
H L K X E B S E B C E E
X Y Q I D B P D I M S X
G B D I C R V U T F H S
U U S K E S Q I E K Q O
R K M S N O U K Z L K U
T F A M Q O K I W U K A
M G O I I S M N H X S P
E L K W D Z R A U P M T
K J Y G J O P M E R I F
N Y Z J K P K F S S T Z
```

Huge sea monsters have been reported for thousands of years.

They may have been some type of giant sea-going dinosaur, but historians say that giant squid or whales are what sailors usually observed.

One of the most famous monsters was called the Kraken—a creature capable of dragging the largest ships to the bottom of the ocean!

18

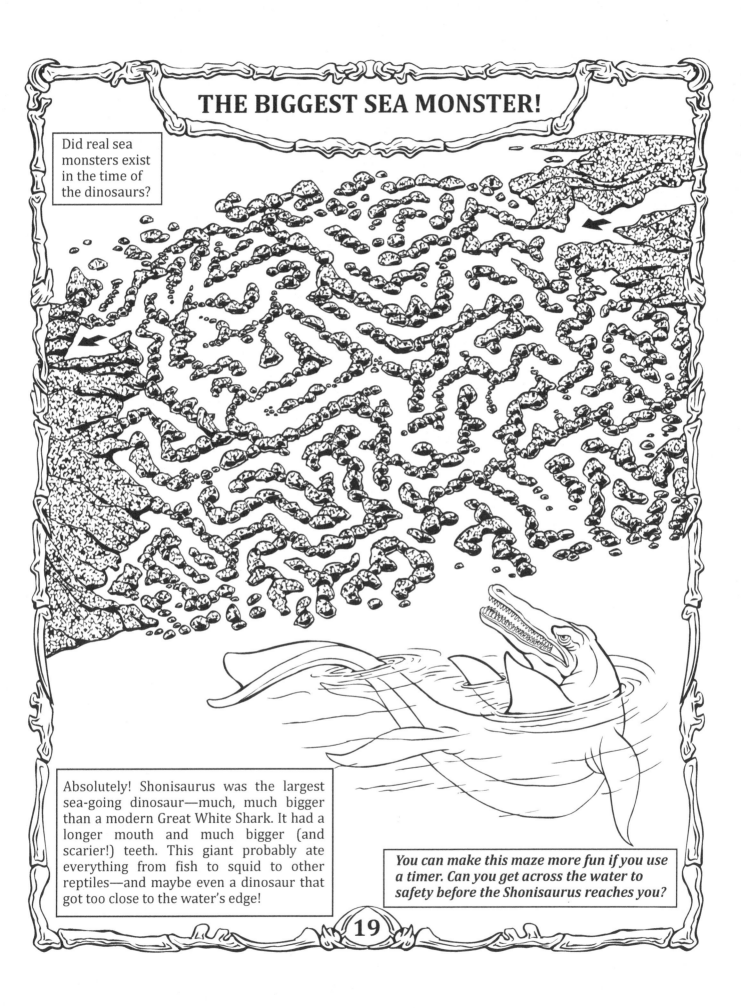

THE BIGGEST SEA MONSTER!

Did real sea monsters exist in the time of the dinosaurs?

Absolutely! Shonisaurus was the largest sea-going dinosaur—much, much bigger than a modern Great White Shark. It had a longer mouth and much bigger (and scarier!) teeth. This giant probably ate everything from fish to squid to other reptiles—and maybe even a dinosaur that got too close to the water's edge!

You can make this maze more fun if you use a timer. Can you get across the water to safety before the Shonisaurus reaches you?

SMALLEST FLYING DINOSAUR EVER!

In 2008, scientists discovered the unusual fossil of Nemi-colopterus, the smallest flying dinosaur ever found! It had a wingspan of only 10 inches and weighed a few ounces. What's amazing about this pigeon-sized creature is that it was in the same family as the winged dinosaur on the next page—the biggest ever: the enormous Quetzalcoatlus!

Here are seven Nemicolopterus. Two are exactly the same. Find and circle them.

BIGGEST FLYING DINOSAUR EVER!

Named after the Aztec feathered snake god Quetzalcoatl, Quetzalcoatlus was discovered in Texas in 1971 when fossils were found of a partial wing from a flying creature the size of a small airplane! It was so big that it must have flown super-long distances—which explains why the same types of fossils were found on the other side of the planet.

Unscramble the names of other flying reptiles:

**PTERODACTYL, NEMICOLOPTERUS, QUETZALCOATLUS, HATZEGOPTERYX
PTERANODON, RHAMPHORHYNCHUS, PTERODAUSTRO**

1. YHHHRSACPRUOHMN _____

2. CLUEQAALSTOTZU _____

3. ATYRCLETDOP _____

4. NONTEPAODR _____

5. EHGYAOTRZEPXT _____

6. TOLMNRUEPECOSI _____

7. UEDPROTTSAOR _____

BIRD OR DINOSAUR—OR BOTH?

Some scientists think that Dromaeosaurs could be the closest relatives to modern birds. Dromaeosaurus was the original raptor— a small, vicious hunter that had a mouth full of razor-sharp teeth. Like modern-day eagles and hawks, it had feathers, keen eyesight and hearing, and a secret weapon: at the end of its powerful legs were two curved toes and a strange-looking claw, used to kill its prey, on top of the foot. Dromaeosaurs grew to be approximately six feet in length and weighed about 33 pounds. It probably was the size of a large dog. But how did smaller dinosaurs like the Dromaeosaur survive among the giants? They hunted in packs to survive. One raptor alone wasn't strong enough, but a group of them could bring down a much bigger animal—like modern day wolves or jackals.

WEIRD HEADS!

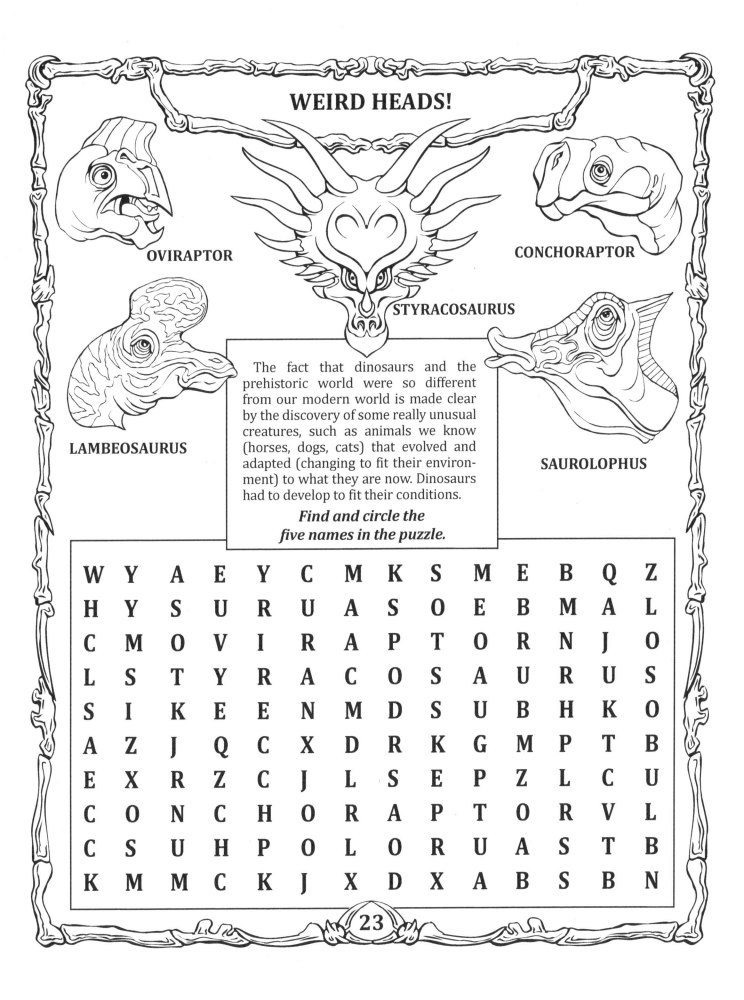

OVIRAPTOR

CONCHORAPTOR

STYRACOSAURUS

LAMBEOSAURUS

SAUROLOPHUS

The fact that dinosaurs and the prehistoric world were so different from our modern world is made clear by the discovery of some really unusual creatures, such as animals we know (horses, dogs, cats) that evolved and adapted (changing to fit their environment) to what they are now. Dinosaurs had to develop to fit their conditions.

Find and circle the five names in the puzzle.

W	Y	A	E	Y	C	M	K	S	M	E	B	Q	Z
H	Y	S	U	R	U	A	S	O	E	B	M	A	L
C	M	O	V	I	R	A	P	T	O	R	N	J	O
L	S	T	Y	R	A	C	O	S	A	U	R	U	S
S	I	K	E	E	N	M	D	S	U	B	H	K	O
A	Z	J	Q	C	X	D	R	K	G	M	P	T	B
E	X	R	Z	C	J	L	S	E	P	Z	L	C	U
C	O	N	C	H	O	R	A	P	T	O	R	V	L
C	S	U	H	P	O	L	O	R	U	A	S	T	B
K	M	M	C	K	J	X	D	X	A	B	S	B	N

UNEVEN DINOSAUR?

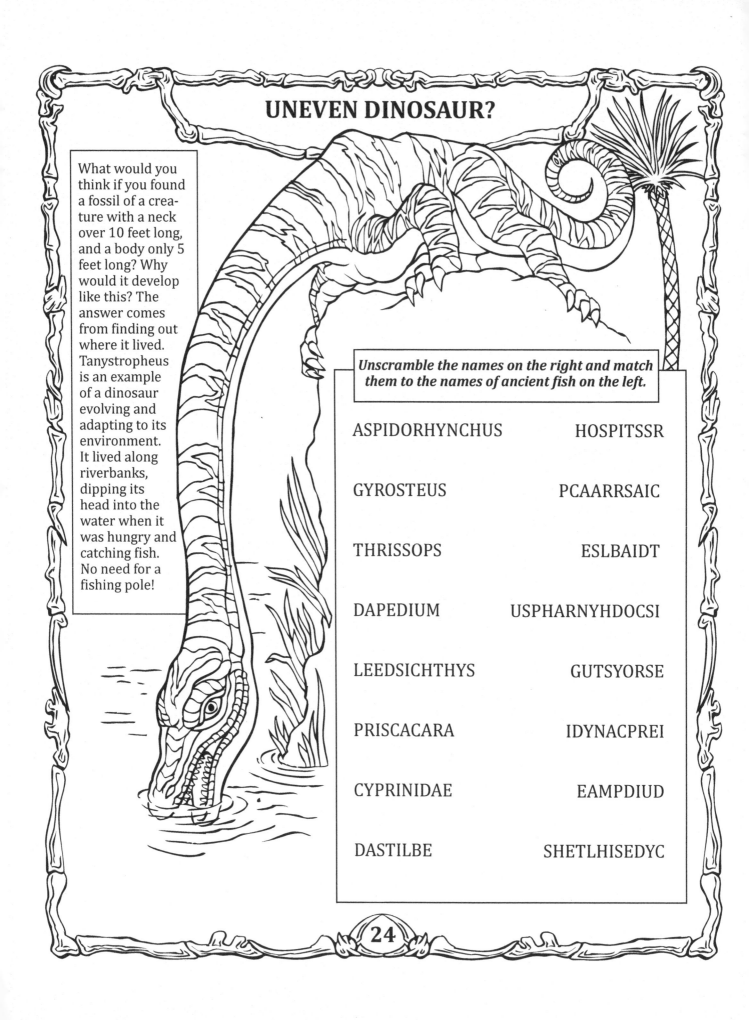

What would you think if you found a fossil of a creature with a neck over 10 feet long, and a body only 5 feet long? Why would it develop like this? The answer comes from finding out where it lived. Tanystropheus is an example of a dinosaur evolving and adapting to its environment. It lived along riverbanks, dipping its head into the water when it was hungry and catching fish. No need for a fishing pole!

Unscramble the names on the right and match them to the names of ancient fish on the left.

ASPIDORHYNCHUS   HOSPITSSR

GYROSTEUS   PCAARRSAIC

THRISSOPS   ESLBAIDT

DAPEDIUM   USPHARNYHDOCSI

LEEDSICHTHYS   GUTSYORSE

PRISCACARA   IDYNACPREI

CYPRINIDAE   EAMPDIUD

DASTILBE   SHETLHISEDYC

24

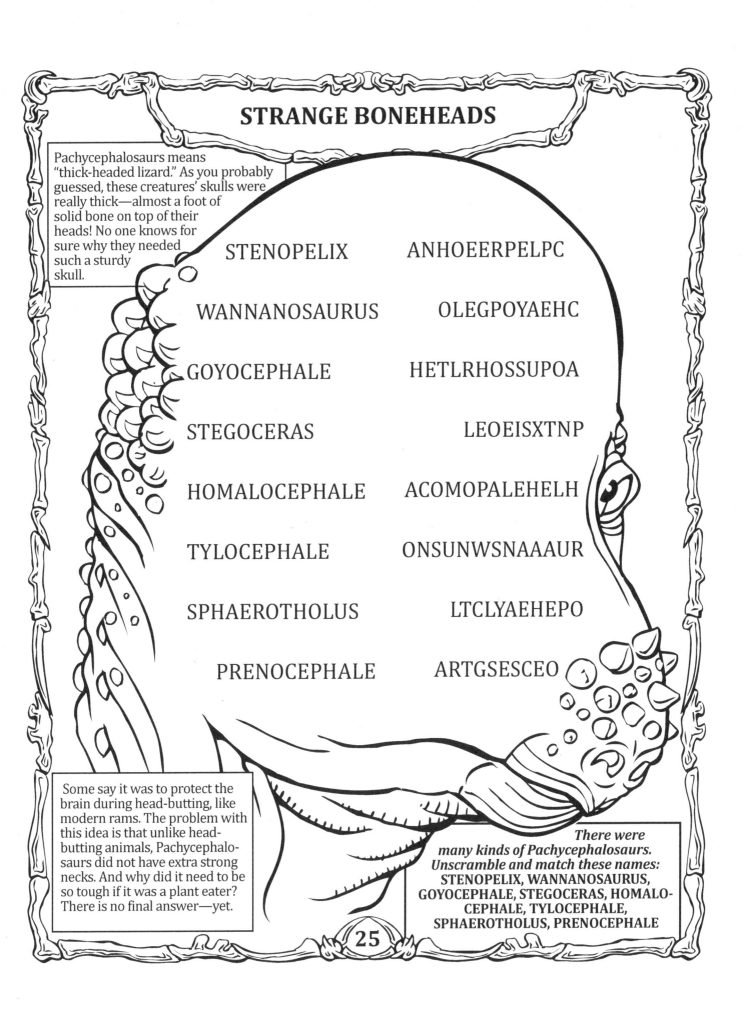

STRANGE BONEHEADS

Pachycephalosaurs means "thick-headed lizard." As you probably guessed, these creatures' skulls were really thick—almost a foot of solid bone on top of their heads! No one knows for sure why they needed such a sturdy skull.

STENOPELIX
WANNANOSAURUS
GOYOCEPHALE
STEGOCERAS
HOMALOCEPHALE
TYLOCEPHALE
SPHAEROTHOLUS
PRENOCEPHALE

ANHOEERPELPC
OLEGPOYAEHC
HETLRHOSSUPOA
LEOEISXTNP
ACOMOPALEHELH
ONSUNWSNAAAUR
LTCLYAEHEPO
ARTGSESCEO

Some say it was to protect the brain during head-butting, like modern rams. The problem with this idea is that unlike head-butting animals, Pachycephalosaurs did not have extra strong necks. And why did it need to be so tough if it was a plant eater? There is no final answer—yet.

There were many kinds of Pachycephalosaurs. Unscramble and match these names: **STENOPELIX, WANNANOSAURUS, GOYOCEPHALE, STEGOCERAS, HOMALOCEPHALE, TYLOCEPHALE, SPHAEROTHOLUS, PRENOCEPHALE**

FLYING VAMPIRE?

Most flying dinosaurs had long, narrow, dangerous-looking beaks. Not the mysterious Jeholopterus, though! It didn't look like any other winged dinosaur. Its face was more cat-like, with double-fanged jaws. So why did it have a flat nose and pointy teeth? Some scientists believe that Jeholopterus was just like a vampire bat, biting large dinosaurs and sucking their blood. Ouch!

Can you find and circle ten differences?

26

STRANGE FOSSIL

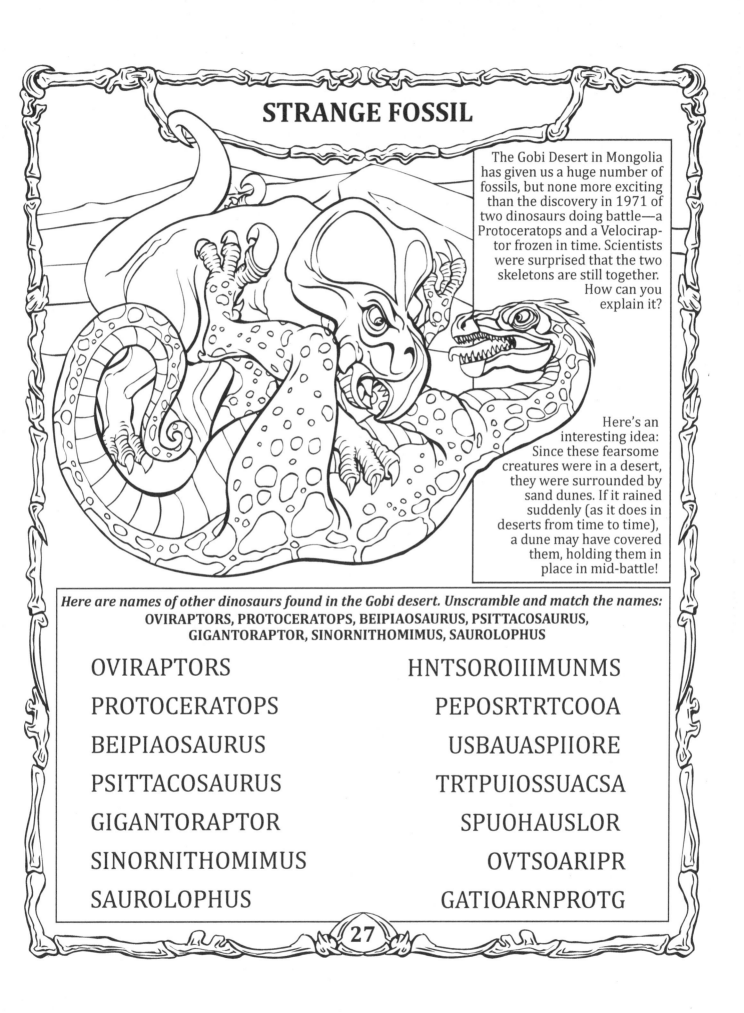

The Gobi Desert in Mongolia has given us a huge number of fossils, but none more exciting than the discovery in 1971 of two dinosaurs doing battle—a Protoceratops and a Velociraptor frozen in time. Scientists were surprised that the two skeletons are still together. How can you explain it?

Here's an interesting idea: Since these fearsome creatures were in a desert, they were surrounded by sand dunes. If it rained suddenly (as it does in deserts from time to time), a dune may have covered them, holding them in place in mid-battle!

Here are names of other dinosaurs found in the Gobi desert. Unscramble and match the names:
OVIRAPTORS, PROTOCERATOPS, BEIPIAOSAURUS, PSITTACOSAURUS, GIGANTORAPTOR, SINORNITHOMIMUS, SAUROLOPHUS

OVIRAPTORS	HNTSOROIIIMUNMS
PROTOCERATOPS	PEPOSRTRTCOOA
BEIPIAOSAURUS	USBAUASPIIORE
PSITTACOSAURUS	TRTPUIOSSUACSA
GIGANTORAPTOR	SPUOHAUSLOR
SINORNITHOMIMUS	OVTSOARIPR
SAUROLOPHUS	GATIOARNPROTG

BUILT LIKE A TANK?

The Ankylosaurus must have been an awesome sight! Covered in armor plate and horns, with a big bone hammer at the end of its tail, it must have made predators think twice about getting too close! But how strong was the armor? Modern animals like crocodiles and armadillos have a kind of tough skin covering, but what about dinosaurs? Scientists began to study the armor of the Ankylosaurus and found that it matched the strength of a modern bulletproof vest! It was the best-protected creature to have ever walked the Earth.

One scientist said: "Other dinosaurs would have to be really hungry to want to attack an Ankylosaurus."

DID DINOSAURS TRAVEL FAR?

Many modern animals migrate (that is, travel long distances to find a home) and scientists wondered whether the dinosaurs did, too.

Can you find your way through the mountains to the plains?

By comparing fossils found in different areas and matching them, they found that some polar dinosaurs like the Edmontosaurus were able to travel over 1,000 miles to find warmer areas. Smaller dinosaurs did not seem to travel as much.

WERE DINOSAURS SMART?

Troodons (meaning "wounding tooth") were small predator dinosaurs (6 feet long) with big claws and saw-like teeth. Troodons had the best vision of any dinosaur and a big brain for its size, making it one of the smartest dinosaurs, too! Troodons were fast, making it hard for their prey to escape from them!

Can you escape through the forest and avoid the Troodons?

THE STRANGE STEGOSAURUS

Stegosaurus had 17 bony plates on its back. No one was sure what the plates were for, or in what order they fit, until 1992, when a nearly complete skeleton was found in Colorado. So what were the bony plates for? Protection? Balance? Scientists believe they have found the answer: The plates controlled the temperature in Stegosaurus's body to keep it from overheating. Stegosaurus also had spikes at the end of its flexible tail. These spikes were up to four feet long and were used for protection from predators.

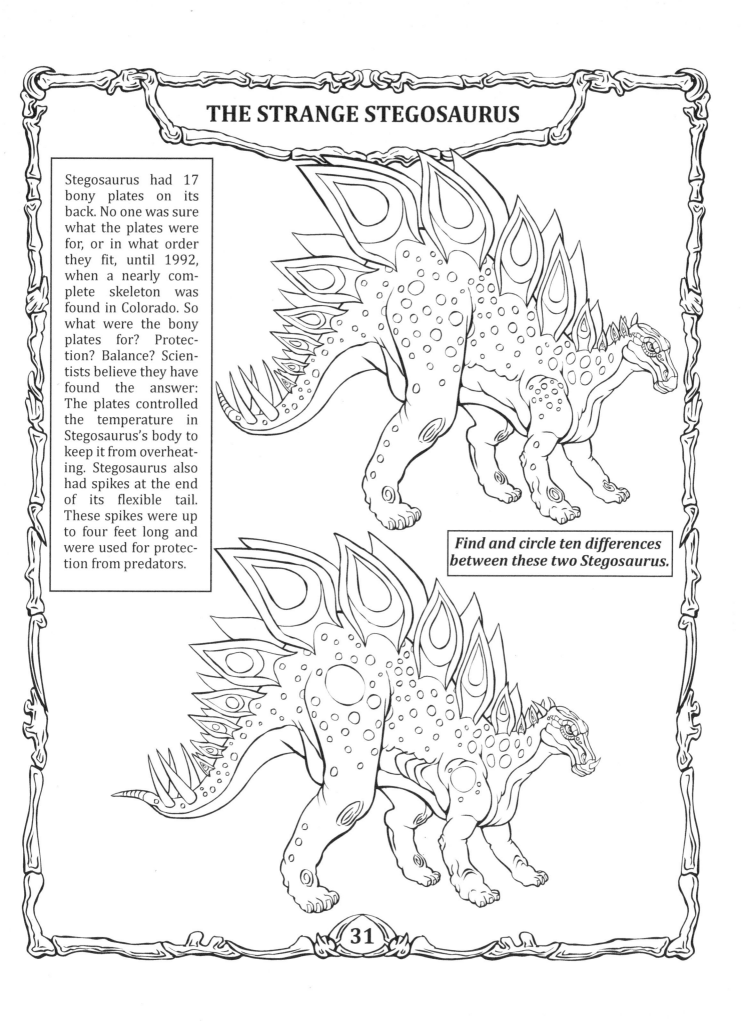

Find and circle ten differences between these two Stegosaurus.

STOLEN DINOSAUR EGGS?

The first dinosaur egg fossils were found in France in 1869. Dinosaur eggs came in many shapes and sizes, some almost two feet long. Large eggs didn't always mean large dinosaurs, though—some very large dinosaurs had small eggs. In 2006, a mystery needed to be solved, and the FBI contacted a scientist from Alberta, Canada (home of Dinosaur Park) to help solve it. More than four tons of stolen fossils had to be returned, but to where? After eight months, the scientist had solved the crime—by studying stolen dinosaur eggs. Their home was in Argentina!

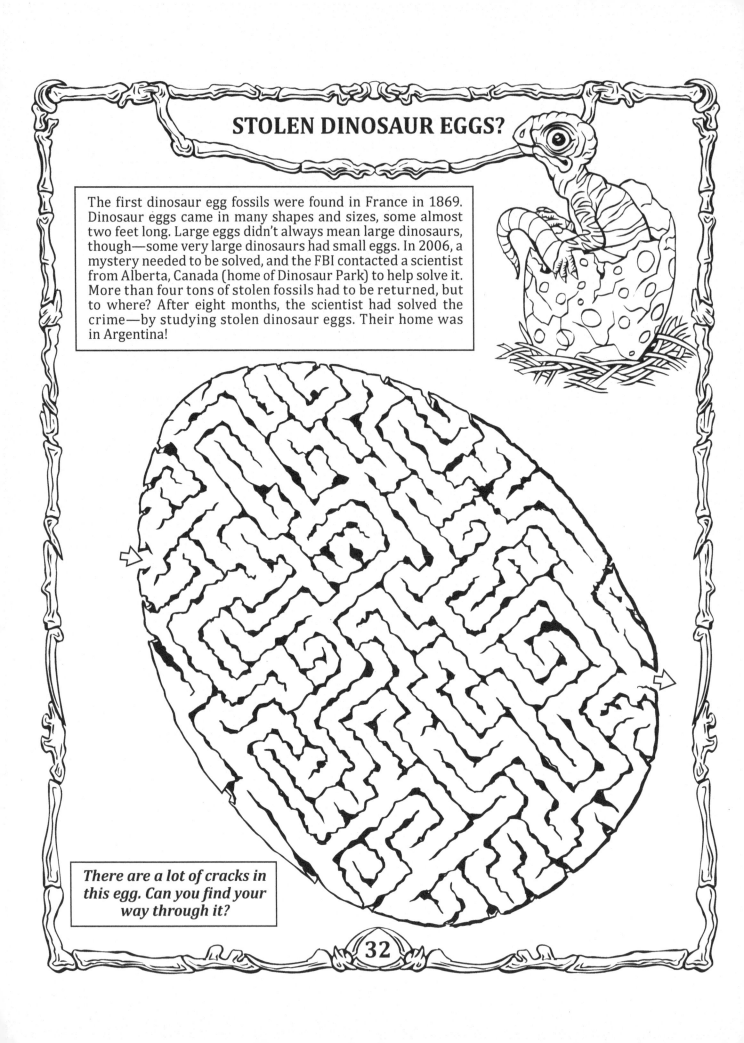

There are a lot of cracks in this egg. Can you find your way through it?

HORN OR THUMB?

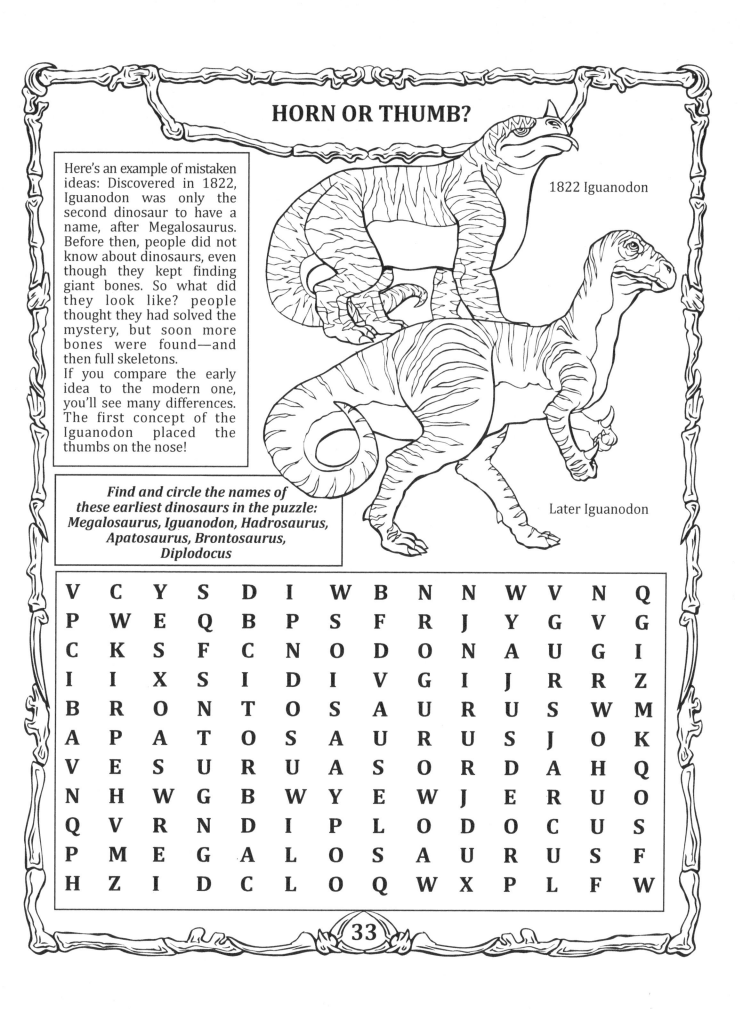

Here's an example of mistaken ideas: Discovered in 1822, Iguanodon was only the second dinosaur to have a name, after Megalosaurus. Before then, people did not know about dinosaurs, even though they kept finding giant bones. So what did they look like? people thought they had solved the mystery, but soon more bones were found—and then full skeletons.

If you compare the early idea to the modern one, you'll see many differences. The first concept of the Iguanodon placed the thumbs on the nose!

1822 Iguanodon

Later Iguanodon

Find and circle the names of these earliest dinosaurs in the puzzle: Megalosaurus, Iguanodon, Hadrosaurus, Apatosaurus, Brontosaurus, Diplodocus

V	C	Y	S	D	I	W	B	N	N	W	V	N	Q
P	W	E	Q	B	P	S	F	R	J	Y	G	V	G
C	K	S	F	C	N	O	D	O	N	A	U	G	I
I	I	X	S	I	D	I	V	G	I	J	R	R	Z
B	R	O	N	T	O	S	A	U	R	U	S	W	M
A	P	A	T	O	S	A	U	R	U	S	J	O	K
V	E	S	U	R	U	A	S	O	R	D	A	H	Q
N	H	W	G	B	W	Y	E	W	J	E	R	U	O
Q	V	R	N	D	I	P	L	O	D	O	C	U	S
P	M	E	G	A	L	O	S	A	U	R	U	S	F
H	Z	I	D	C	L	O	Q	W	X	P	L	F	W

THE GREAT DINOSAUR RACE

An amazing thing happened in the United States at the end of the nineteenth century. Fossils of dinosaurs were being discovered almost daily! In a short while, museums and colleges were busy building skeletons and naming these new dinosaurs—but why the hurry? Researchers seemed to be in a race to see who would find the most and best fossils. Who was behind this mystery? It all began with an argument between two famous scientists, E. D. Cope and O. C. Marsh, over where a skull should go on a skeleton! The race was on, and in the end they had discovered and named almost 130 dinosaurs.

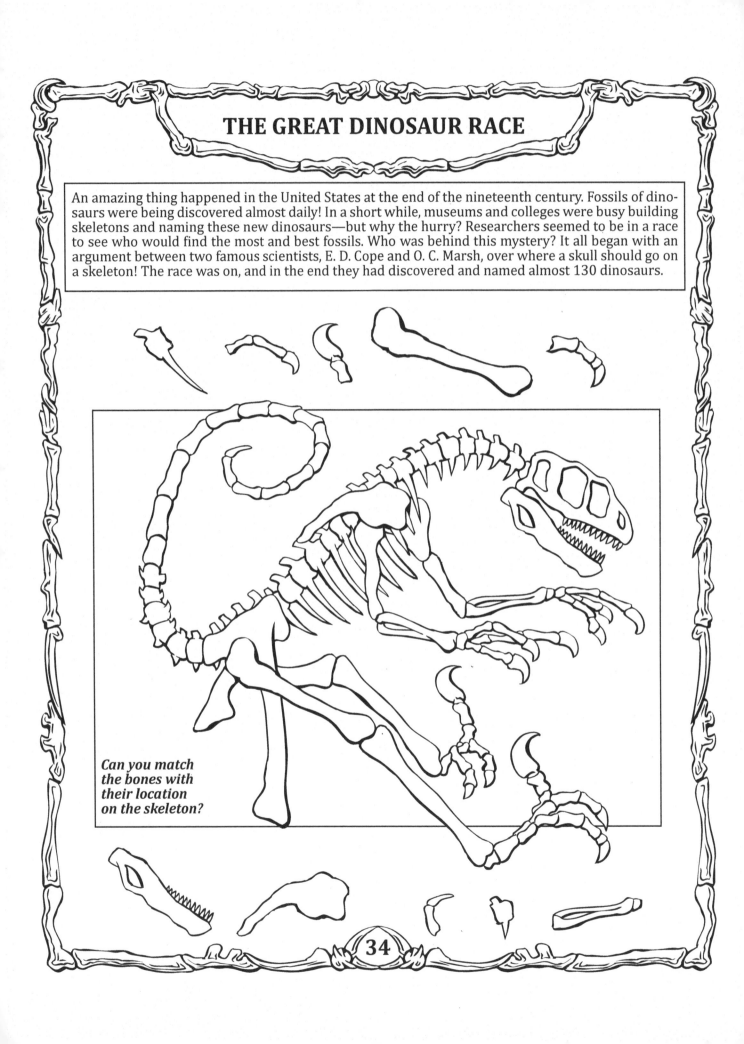

Can you match the bones with their location on the skeleton?

WHAT HAPPENED TO THE DINOSAURS?

Scientists have tried to find a reason for the disappearance of the dinosaurs. Some said it was a contagious illness or suddenly changing weather. These are interesting ideas, but most experts agree that the cause would have to be something big and powerful!

35

EARTHLY END?

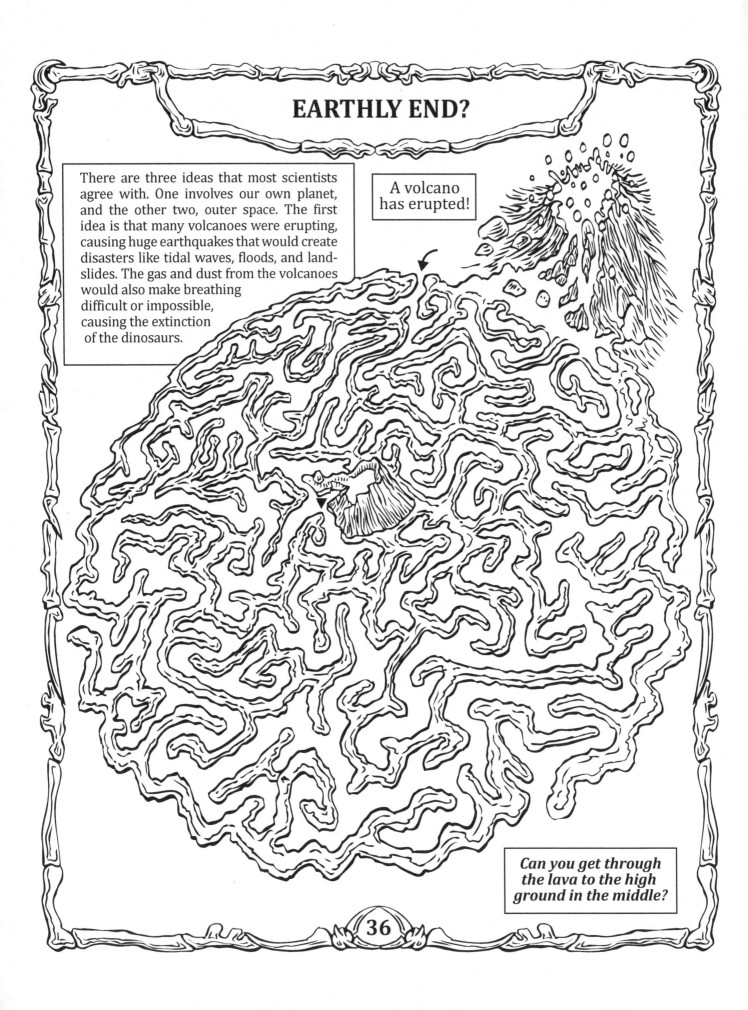

There are three ideas that most scientists agree with. One involves our own planet, and the other two, outer space. The first idea is that many volcanoes were erupting, causing huge earthquakes that would create disasters like tidal waves, floods, and landslides. The gas and dust from the volcanoes would also make breathing difficult or impossible, causing the extinction of the dinosaurs.

A volcano has erupted!

Can you get through the lava to the high ground in the middle?

DEEP FREEZE

Many scientists say that an asteroid or a comet from space upset the balance of the Earth, causing the planet to go into a deep freeze. Some scientists believe that this major drop in temperature caused the cold-blooded dinosaurs to die out, while the warm-blooded mammals were able to survive. All of the plant, animal, and marine life that could not adapt to the cold temperatures became extinct.

Here are names of prehistoric mammals that came out of the Ice Age. Find them in the puzzle.

BRONTOTHERIUM, MAMMOTH, CORYPHODON, SMILODON, TOXODON, HYRACOTHERIUM

```
D  D  M  M  H  O  G  N  O  G  O  S  I  S  R  I
E  B  R  G  U  T  U  I  O  A  X  T  I  R  C  A
E  F  R  Q  I  I  O  R  Z  D  O  L  X  Z  T  J
E  R  B  D  M  U  R  M  K  X  O  U  C  S  T  H
X  T  J  E  G  Z  P  R  E  M  A  M  X  C  Y  Y
X  F  I  X  Z  Z  C  C  H  A  E  Q  O  R  P  H
A  X  V  G  U  O  P  Z  L  T  M  N  A  T  L  O
F  E  B  V  G  H  O  N  Z  O  O  C  Y  Z  R  G
I  X  P  E  H  H  P  O  B  D  O  T  L  D  H  M
D  G  B  L  Q  W  D  V  O  T  B  A  N  Y  Z  V
O  G  T  C  B  O  A  H  H  T  K  O  S  O  V  P
M  O  W  H  L  P  P  E  K  V  Z  I  W  S  R  A
M  V  E  I  S  Y  R  N  W  U  B  G  S  D  B  H
V  C  M  Q  R  I  X  M  W  U  O  I  G  Q  M  B
C  S  E  O  U  Z  F  O  O  L  P  K  W  J  O  V
Z  V  C  M  F  C  Z  K  J  T  Y  F  X  D  I  M
```

TERROR FROM SPACE

The other idea that most scientists agree with is that a giant meteor or asteroid crashed into the earth, causing earthquakes, tidal waves, and floods.

Unscramble the names of these crash sites and write them on the lines.

THE NORTH SEA, WEST QUEBEC, HUDSON'S BAY, GULF OF MEXICO, THE ARAL SEA, TAJIKISTAN, SOUTH AFRICA, AUSTRALIA

1. HREAOTEHSNT _____

2. OXULMEFGIOCF_____

3. EQUEEWBSTC _____

4. STAKINAJIT _____

5. AIRUTASLA _____

6. BDSYHUNSAO _____

7. UHFSTOAIACR _____

8. EEAHAALRST _____

A LOST WORLD

The dinosaurs have left us enough physical evidence to excite our imagination and encourage us to learn more about our wonderful world and its mysteries.

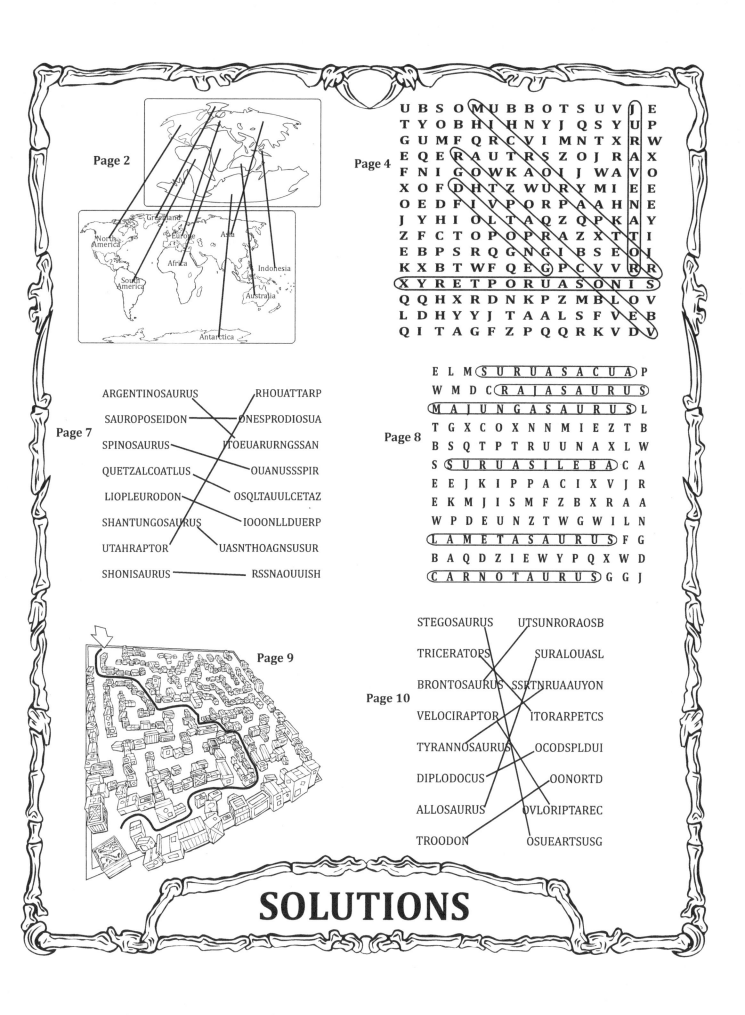

Page 2

Page 4

```
U B S O M U B B O T S U V J E
T Y O B H I H N Y J Q S Y U P
G U M F Q R C V I M N T X R W
E Q E R A U T R S Z O J R A X
F N I G O W K A O I J W A V O
X O D H T Z W U R Y M I E N E
O E D F I V P O R P A A H N E
J Y H I O L T A Q Z Q P K A Y
Z F C T O P O P R A Z X T T I
E B P S R Q G N G I B S E O I
K X B T W F Q E G P C V V R R
X Y R E T P O R U A S O N I S
Q Q H X R D N K P Z M B L O V
L D H Y Y J T A A L S F V E B
Q I T A G F Z P Q Q R K V D V
```

Page 7

ARGENTINOSAURUS — RHOUATTARP
SAUROPOSEIDON — ONESPRODIOSUA
SPINOSAURUS — ITOEUARURNGSSAN
QUETZALCOATLUS — OUANUSSSPIR
LIOPLEURODON — OSQLTAUULCETAZ
SHANTUNGOSAURUS — IOOONLLDUERP
UTAHRAPTOR — UASNTHOAGNSUSUR
SHONISAURUS — RSSNAOUUISH

Page 8

```
E L M S U R U A S A C U A P
W M D C R A J A S A U R U S
M A J U N G A S A U R U S L
T G X C O X N N M I E Z T B
B S Q T P T R U U N A X L W
S S U R U A S I L E B A C A
E E J K I P P A C I X V J R
E K M J I S M F Z B X R A A
W P D E U N Z T W G W I L N
L A M E T A S A U R U S F G
B A Q D Z I E W Y P Q X W D
C A R N O T A U R U S G G J
```

Page 9

Page 10

STEGOSAURUS — UTSUNRORAOSB
TRICERATOPS — SURALOUASL
BRONTOSAURUS — SSRTNRUAAUYON
VELOCIRAPTOR — ITORARPETCS
TYRANNOSAURUS — OCODSPLDUI
DIPLODOCUS — OONORTD
ALLOSAURUS — OVLORIPTAREC
TROODON — OSUEARTSUSG

SOLUTIONS

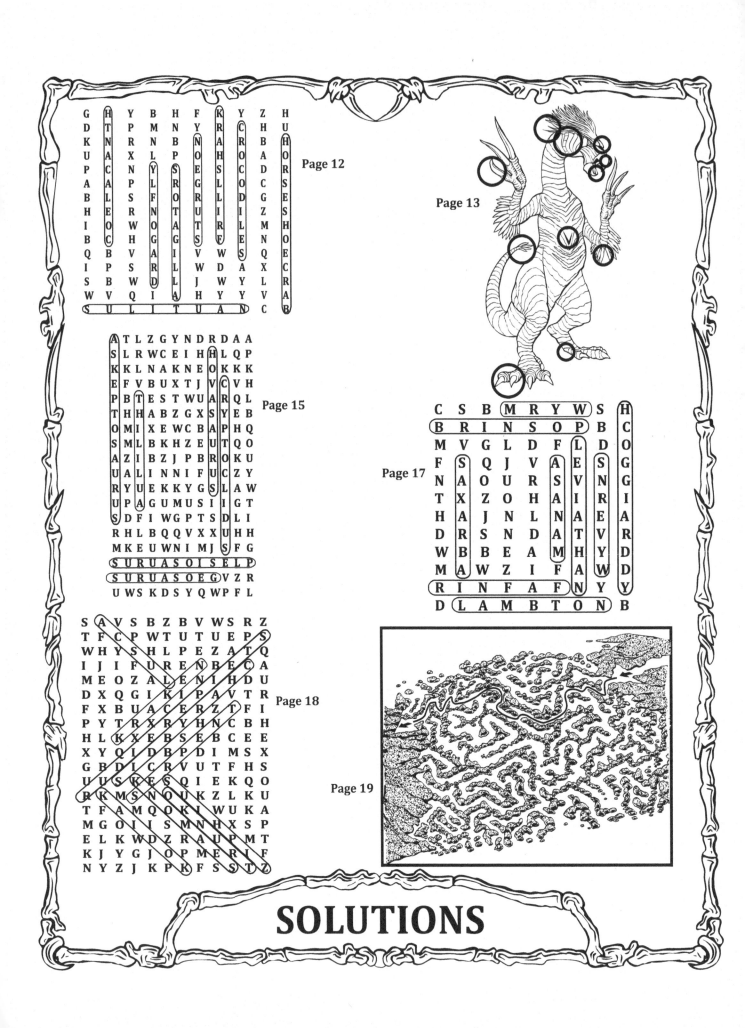

Page 12

Page 13

Page 15

Page 17

Page 18

Page 19

SOLUTIONS

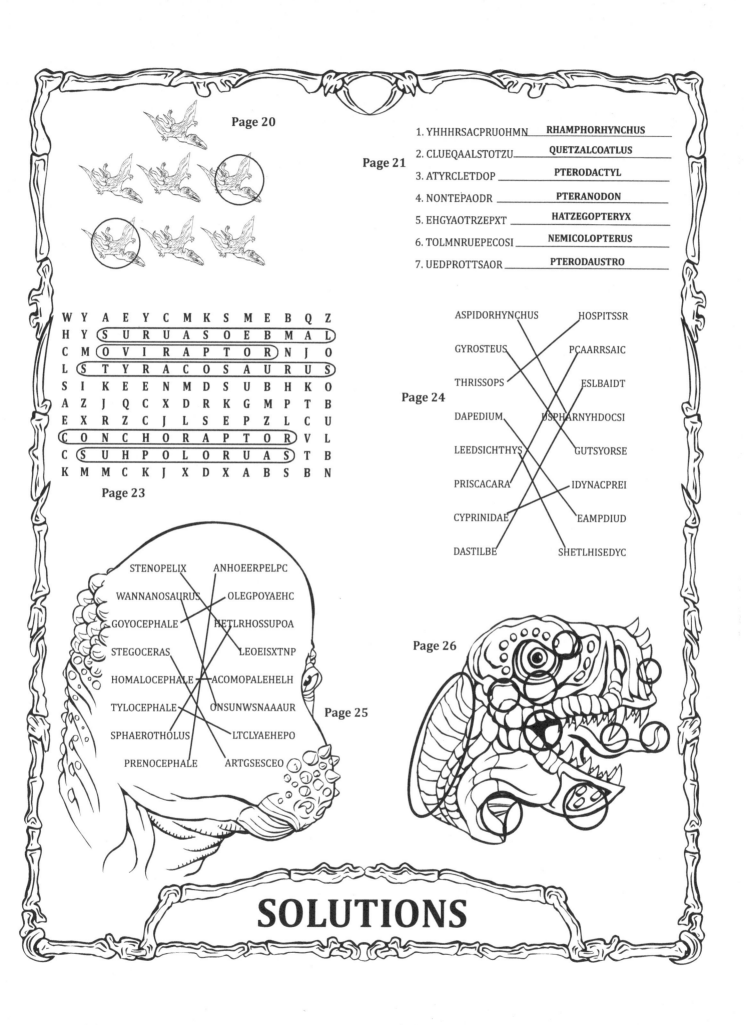

Page 20

Page 21

1. YHHHRSACPRUOHMN — **RHAMPHORHYNCHUS**
2. CLUEQAALSTOTZU — **QUETZALCOATLUS**
3. ATYRCLETDOP — **PTERODACTYL**
4. NONTEPAODR — **PTERANODON**
5. EHGYAOTRZEPXT — **HATZEGOPTERYX**
6. TOLMNRUEPECOSI — **NEMICOLOPTERUS**
7. UEDPROTTSAOR — **PTERODAUSTRO**

Page 23

```
W Y A E Y C M K S M E B Q Z
H Y S U R U A S O E B M A L
C M O V I R A P T O R N J O
L S S T Y R A C O S A U R U S
S I K E E N M D S U B H K O
A Z J Q C X D R K G M P T B
E X R Z C J L S E P Z L C U
C O N C H O R A P T O R V L
C S U H P O L O R U A S T B
K M M C K J X D X A B S B N
```

Page 24

ASPIDORHYNCHUS   HOSPITSSR
GYROSTEUS   PCAARRSAIC
THRISSOPS   ESLBAIDT
DAPEDIUM   USPHARNYHDOCSI
LEEDSICHTHYS   GUTSYORSE
PRISCACARA   IDYNACPREI
CYPRINIDAE   EAMPDIUD
DASTILBE   SHETLHISEDYC

Page 25

STENOPELIX   ANHOEERPELPC
WANNANOSAURUS   OLEGPOYAEHC
GOYOCEPHALE   HETLRHOSSUPOA
STEGOCERAS   LEOEISXTNP
HOMALOCEPHALE   ACOMOPALEHELH
TYLOCEPHALE   ONSUNWSNAAAUR
SPHAEROTHOLUS   LTCLYAEHEPO
PRENOCEPHALE   ARTGSESCEO

Page 26

SOLUTIONS

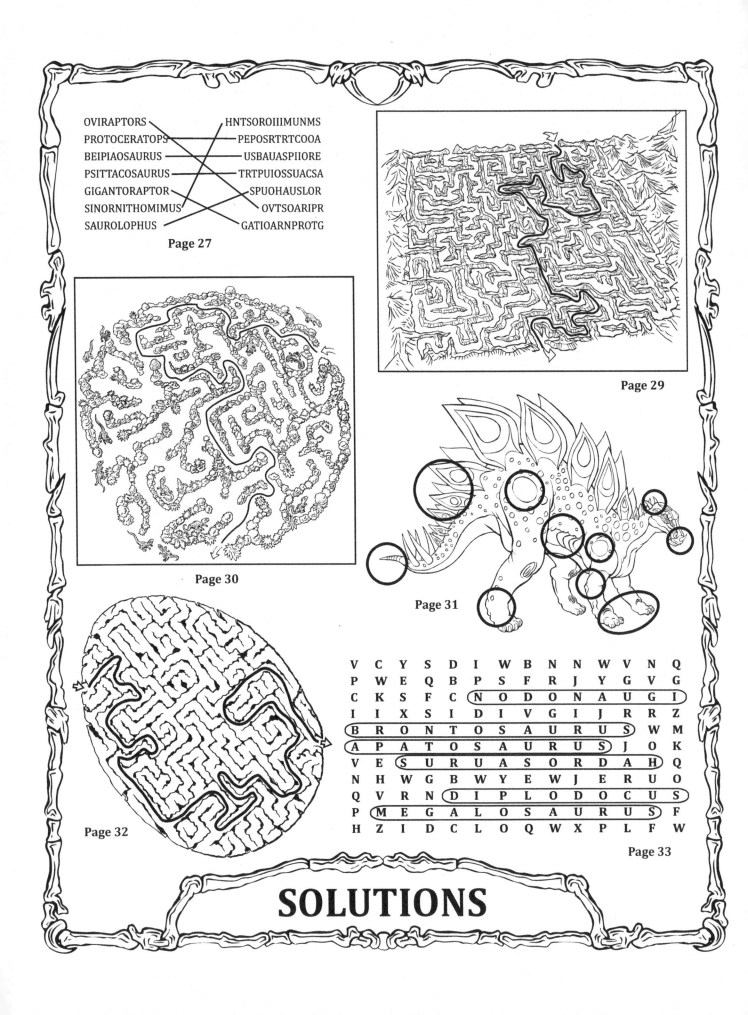

OVIRAPTORS
PROTOCERATOPS
BEIPIAOSAURUS
PSITTACOSAURUS
GIGANTORAPTOR
SINORNITHOMIMUS
SAUROLOPHUS

HNTSOROIIIMUNMS
PEPOSRTRTCOOA
USBAUASPIIORE
TRTPUIOSSUACSA
SPUOHAUSLOR
OVTSOARIPR
GATIOARNPROTG

Page 27

Page 29

Page 30

Page 31

Page 32

V	C	Y	S	D	I	W	B	N	N	W	V	N	Q
P	W	E	Q	B	P	S	F	R	J	Y	G	V	G
C	K	S	F	C	N	O	D	O	N	A	U	G	I
I	I	X	S	I	D	I	V	G	I	J	R	R	Z
B	R	O	N	T	O	S	A	U	R	U	S	W	M
A	P	A	T	O	S	A	U	R	U	S	J	O	K
V	E	S	U	R	U	A	S	O	R	D	A	H	Q
N	H	W	G	B	W	Y	E	W	J	E	R	U	O
Q	V	R	N	D	I	P	L	O	D	O	C	U	S
P	M	E	G	A	L	O	S	A	U	R	U	S	F
H	Z	I	D	C	L	O	Q	W	X	P	L	F	W

Page 33

SOLUTIONS

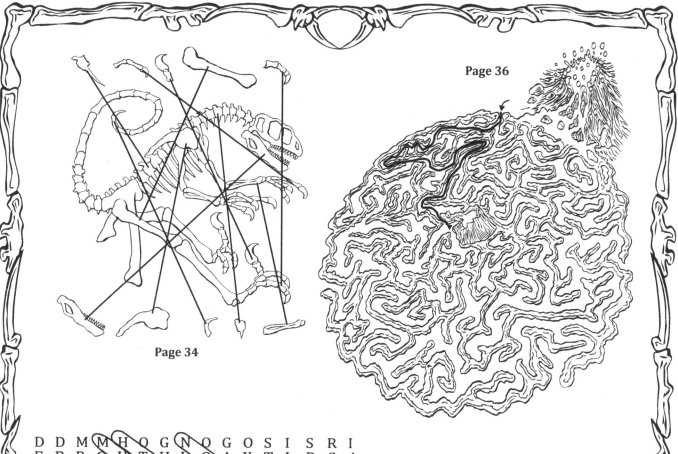

Page 36

Page 34

D D M M H O G N O G O S I S R I
E B R G U T U I O A X T I X S R C T I A L
E F R Q D I R Z D O L U C S R T Y I H
X R B I M U R M K X O U Z C S T Y P H O
X T F E G Z P R E M A M X I Z Q R L G M
A J I X U O C P Z L T M N A T Y R H V K
A X E G V V G H O C Q O C I D Z R H Z P A
I X B E H H P O B O O T L D H V K P H
D G B L Q W D V O T B A N Y Z O V A H
O O T C B O A H H T K O S O V R B V B
M W H L P P E K V Z I W S D B
M V E I S Y R N W U B G S D B
C M Q R I X M W U O I K G Q B M O I
C S E Q U Z F O O L P J W J M C
Z V C M F C Z K J T Y F X D I M C

Page 37

1. HREAOTEHSNT **THE NORTH SEA**

2. OXULMEFGIOCF **GULF OF MEXICO**

3. EQUEEWBSTC **WEST QUEBEC**

4. STAKINAJIT **TAJIKISTAN**

5. AIRUTASLA **AUSTRALIA**

6. BDSYHUNSAO **HUDSON'S BAY**

7. UHFSTOAIACR **SOUTH AFRICA**

8. EEAHAALRST **THE ARAL SEA**

Page 38

SOLUTIONS